# Healing

# JOURNAL

## GOD'S WORD:
The Tree *of* Life

# ETHELENE
# STANLEY

**CREATION
HOUSE**

40 Day Healing Journal by Ethelene Stanley
Published by Creation House
A Charisma Media Company
600 Rinehart Road
Lake Mary, Florida 32746
www.charismamedia.com

Unless otherwise noted, all Scripture quotations are from the King James Version of the Bible.

Scripture quotations marked NKJV are from the New King James Version of the Bible. Copyright © 1979, 1980, 1982 by Thomas Nelson, Inc., publishers. Used by permission.

Scripture quotations marked AMP are from the Amplified Bible. Old Testament copyright © 1965, 1987 by the Zondervan Corporation. The Amplified New Testament copyright © 1954, 1958, 1987 by the Lockman Foundation. Used by permission.

Design Director: Bill Johnson
Cover design by Terry Clifton and Jason Ward

Library of Congress Cataloging-in-Publication Data: 2013937678
International Standard Book Number: 978-1-62136-365-1
E-book International Standard Book Number: 978-1-62136-366-8

While the author has made every effort to provide accurate telephone numbers and Internet addresses at the time of publication, neither the publisher nor the author assumes any responsibility for errors or for changes that occur after publication.

First edition

13 14 15 16 17 — 9 8 7 6 5 4 3 2 1
Printed in Canada

# DEDICATION

*To my wonderful, loving, and
devoted husband, John; thank you
for always believing in me.*

*To my beloved daughters; Corretta,
Charlena, and Mary, for telling me I
could do it, and for encouraging me
to submit this book to be published.*

*To my son-in-law, Jason Ward, for helping
me with the cover design for this book.*

*To my granddaughter, Malika, for helping
me each step of the way. Verna, Margaret,
and Wanda, thank you for your wisdom.*

*To the Holy Spirit, for being my
helper; without You this book
would not have been written.*

*—Thank You*

# TABLE OF CONTENTS

# INTRODUCTION

THIS BOOK IS a lifelong journal searching for the truth about healing. From the age of twelve all I can remember about my family was sickness—cancer, for a matter of fact. When I was about nine, my mother found out she had cancer while pregnant with my youngest sister. A year and a half later, after having my sister, she passed away. As a young child it felt like she went into the hospital and never came home. I just couldn't believe that this God that was so good and loving could take a mother away from her small children—I was number five of fourteen—and I was in disbelief that God could leave us motherless.

This continued to be a constant tragedy in our lives. It was like every other year someone in our immediate family was battling cancer. For a brief time I stopped believing in God.

Each time someone died in our family I had the same questions: What has my family done to God that He wouldn't answer our prayers? Where is this Healer? What do we need to do to receive this healing God promised us?

In 1983, I met this lady who was my daughter's babysitter. Each day when I came to pick my daughter up she would talk to me about God, and how good He is. It was like she reignited my flame for the Lord. I wanted to learn more about Jesus, because she told me I could become a better person, even a better mother, and I wanted to become that woman. After a few months of Bible study, I learned I could really be healed.

So I started this quest to find out why my family was dying in spite of what the Word of God was saying about healing. I began an intense praying session with God, asking Him to reveal to me what was going on with my family.

I began to understand the knowledge of being healed. Over the next few years I started learning and experiencing healing in my body.

My family and I have been through a lot; but God never allowed us to go through anything we couldn't handle with His help.

In 2011 my husband, John, and I went to our annual Kenneth Copeland conference in northern Virginia. Each meeting ended with Gloria ministering on healing. What an eye-opening experience. At the conference I learned that healing is for the body of Christ, and that Jesus died for our completeness—not just our salvation, but healing also. When Jesus said, "It is finished," He meant that He had broken the curse and Satan could no longer hold the curse over us. I learned we have a part to play in becoming totally free from curses. I learned that generational curses have a lot to do with sickness; also, holding offense and not walking in love will cause sickness to come upon you.

At the end of the conference, I purchased a book called *Healing Wellness—Your 10 Day Spiritual Action Plan* by Kenneth and Gloria Copeland. WOW, what a book. With this book, along with other books I had been reading and studying, my eyes were opened about the word of healing. Each time I would read and discover new revelations about healing, I would always say, "God, someone needs to teach this here in my area." Then one day God made it clear to me I am the one to teach this information that I have learned and walked in for many years. I knew I had my work cut out for me.

When I made up my mind to teach the class on healing, I looked for a journal to help me with my lessons. After not finding one that I liked specifically focused on healing, I decided to create one for my class. I know this was from the Lord because I am not a writer, but He (God) just poured into me everything I wanted to say and the way to put it. I would go to the table and I felt like God would meet me there. The anointing had an overwhelming feeling; the presence of God was awesome. Some nights I didn't want to leave—even if I was getting tired, I didn't want to stop. I didn't want the presence of God to leave. While I was writing in my journal, God would give me the lessons I needed to teach. He would show me things in His Word I had not seen before.

This journal is a tool; God wants us to use this tool to get us started in our faith walk to receive complete healing. God is the author of this journal; He just used my hands to write what He wants His children to know about healing. This is just the beginning if you let God lead you.

GOD DESIRES FOR us to be healed and whole even more than we desire it. We shouldn't have to twist God's arm to get Him to heal us. His Word says, "Beloved, I wish above all things that thou mayest proper and be in health, even as thy soul prospereth" (3 John 2).

Faith is the force that comes out of your heart and causes the power of God to come into your circumstances.

From the beginning God has desired the very best for His people, including divine health. In Exodus 15:26, God told the children of Israel, "I Am the Lord that healeth thee." With those words, He declared Himself to be our healer.

If He was the Lord who heals, He still is the Lord who heals, because God never changes (James 1:17; Mal. 3:6).

The Lord God is gracious and full of compassion. He is good to all and His tender mercies are over all His words (Ps. 145:8–9); Psalm 107:20 says, "He sent His word, and healed them, and delivered them from their destructions."

The covenant of healing God gave Israel was immunity from disease. He said, "And ye shall serve the LORD your God, and he shall bless thy bread, and thy water; and I will take sickness away from the midst of thee" (Exod. 23:25).

# GOD'S WILL IS FOR YOU TO BE HEALED

MANY HAVE FORGOTTEN God's benefit of healing for our bodies. The bodies of born-again believers are being destroyed because they do not have the knowledge of God's Word. God's will is for us to be healed, but many die young, even though it is not God's will. God said, "I will take sickness away from the midst of thee...the number of thy days I will fulfill" (Exod. 23:25–26). It is not His will for you to die young. It is His will for you to live long and satisfied on the earth without sickness and disease!

**Read: Psalm 103:1–5**

Faith says God can heal. What do you say? What do you believe?

He is the great phy·bat, He also gives a brain to use also!

God wants His people healed. What steps do you need to take to make this happen?

Faith

## Let Us Pray!

*Father, in the name of Jesus I believe that I am healed according to 1 Peter 2:24. Your Word says that Jesus took my infirmities and bore my sickness. Therefore with great boldness and confidence, I stand on the authority of Your Word and declare that I am redeemed from the curse of sickness. I refuse to tolerate its symptoms.*

*In Jesus' name I pray. Amen!*

## DAY 2

# GOD'S GREAT COMMISSION

*Go ye into all the world, and preach the gospel to every crea-
ture. He that believeth and is baptized shall be saved; but
he that believeth not shall be damned. And these signs shall
follow them that believe; in my name shall they cast out devils;
they shall speak with new tongues; they shall take up ser-
pents; and if they drink any deadly thing, it shall not hurt
them; they shall lay hands on the sick, and they shall recover.*
—MARK 16:15–18

**Read: Deuteronomy 7:13–15**

Is this promise for us today? Tell me why?

_____

_____

_____

The Greek and Hebrew word translation of salvation can be asso-
ciated with deliverance, safety, preservation, healing, and health.
What do you think the gospel of Jesus Christ is?

_____

_____

_____

## *Let Us Pray!*

*Dear heavenly Father, I thank You for my salvation. Since I am no longer under the curse of the law, I am free from the curse of sickness and disease. The Lord is faithful to heal all of my diseases. He removes my sickness and restores me to complete health and wellness.*

*In Jesus' name I pray. Amen!*

# I GIVE YOU THE AUTHORITY
# TO RULE THE EARTH

A STORM HAD ARISEN on the Sea of Galilee and Jesus was in the back of the ship asleep on a pillow. The disciples woke Him and said, "Master, carest thou not that we perish?" (Mark 4:38). They thought they were going down at sea. But Jesus arose and rebuked the wind. Jesus wasn't rebuking something God had done; He was rebuking something the devil had stirred up.

**Read: 2 Peter 1:2–6**

Are you able to rebuke the storms in your life? Do you have the authority to rebuke?

_____

_____

_____

What has the devil stirred up in your life? How can you stop it?

_____

_____

_____

## *Let Us Pray!*

*Father, I come boldly to the throne to obtain grace to help in time of need. I have confidence in Your Word, and I take hold of Your promises to heal me, according to Isaiah 53:5 and 1 Peter 2:24. Your Word says that Jesus bore all my sickness and diseases, and carried my sorrows, so I receive healing now. I declare that Jesus is my healer. I give You all the praise for providing everything I need to walk in wholeness. Satan, I declare to you in the name of Jesus that you have no authority over me. According to Matthew 18:18, I bind you from operating against me in any way.*

*In Jesus' name I pray. Amen!*

# KEEP THEM IN THE MIDST
# OF YOUR HEART

Allow God's Word to abide in you by meditating and acting on what you hear. The portion of God's Word that you act on is the portion of His Word that is alive in you. Continually feed yourself with God's Word in order to keep the Word producing the force of faith in you. The Word of God is medicine to you (Prov. 4:20–22).

> It is the Spirit who gave life; the flesh profits nothing. The words I speak unto you are Spirit, and they are life.
>
> —John 6:63

**Read: Proverbs 4:4–6, 20–23**

What is Proverbs 4:20–23 telling you to do?

_____

_____

_____

**Read: Proverbs 12:28**

What is Proverbs 12:28 saying to you?

_____

_____

_____

## *Let Us Pray!*

*Heavenly Father, I attend to Your Word, I incline my ears to Your saying. I will not let them depart from my eyes. I will keep them in the midst of my heart, for they are life and healing to all my flesh. Therefore, I will not allow any sickness to dominate my body. The life of God flows within me, bringing healing and restoring life to me.*

*In Jesus' name I pray. Amen!*

# MAKE GOD'S WORD THE
# FINAL AUTHORITY

THE WORD SAYS that by the stripes of Jesus you were healed (1 Pet. 2:24). Refuse to believe what you see and feel. Only believe the Word. Don't waver; he that wavereth is like a wave of the sea driven with the wind, tossed to and fro and carried about with every wind or doctrine (Eph. 4:14). Therefore, do not cast away your confidence, which has great reward. For you have need of endurance, so that after you have done the will of God, you may receive the promise (Heb. 10:35–36).

**Read: Galatians 3:13; Isaiah 53:4–6**

What do you believe?

_____

_____

_____

**Read: Psalm 91:10–16**

What is Psalm 91 saying?

_____

_____

_____

## Let Us Pray!

*Father, as I study and meditate on Your Word, I am convinced in my heart that You want me to live in health. I know it is Your will. I thank You for working in me as I decide to walk in health, and take action every day.*

*In Jesus' name I pray. Amen!*

# GOD'S WORD: A NEVER FAILING REMEDY

GOD WANTS US to understand the life and power that are in His Word. When God created the earth it was His spoken words that produced the earth.

God's Word is the remedy for all situations and circumstances that may come in our life—that includes sickness and disease.

God's Word will keep you in perfect peace (Isa. 26:3).

Because God's words are full of life and healing, they act as medicine for us if we use them.

The Word won't work for us if we just keep it in our head (Matt. 8:16). The Word needs to get deep inside of us in the spirit, because faith (healing) comes by hearing, and hearing the Word of God (Rom. 10:17).

# GOD'S WORD NEVER FAILS

CERTAINLY NOT! INDEED, let God be true, but every man is a liar. As it is written: "That you may be justified in Your words, and may overcome when you are judged" (Rom. 3:4, NKJV).

> God is not a man that He should lie, nor a son of man, that He should repent. Has He said, and will He not do it? Or has He spoken, and will He not make it good?
> —NUMBERS 23:19, NKJV

**Read: Joshua 21:43–45; 1 Kings 8:56–61**

What has God spoken to you?

_____

_____

_____

Has it come to pass, or is it hung up because of unbelief?

_____

_____

_____

## Let Us Pray!

*Father, in the name of Jesus, I commit myself to walk in the Word. Your Word living in me produces Your life in this world. I recognize that Your Word is integrity itself, steadfast, sure, eternal, and I trust my life to its provisions.*

*In Jesus Christ's name I pray. Amen!*

# THE LANGUAGE OF HEALTH

*For by your words you will be justified, and
by your words you will be condemned.*
—MATTHEW 12:37, NKJV

THE WORDS YOU say will either acquit or condemn you (Matt. 12:34–37). Words can be your salvation or they can damn you. By your words you are healed or you are sick. Wise men store up knowledge, but the mouth of a fool invites ruin (Prov. 10:14). Everyone has heard people say that "by the time you become sixty years old your body starts to fall apart." You are just prophesying your own demise. You need to take authority and dominion over your body with words. "Bless the Lord, O my soul: and all that is within me" (Ps. 103:1–5).

No one has a choice of whether or not they live by words,
but they do have a choice of what words they live by.
—KENNETH COPELAND

**Read: Romans 12:1–2; Romans 13:11–14**

How shall we present our bodies?

_____

_____

_____

What is the good and acceptable will of God?

_____

_____

_____

We must put on the _____  _____

_____ and make not _____ for the flesh,
to fulfill its lusts.

## *Let Us Pray!*

*Father God, as I study and meditate on Your Word, I am convinced in my heart that You want me to live in health. I know it is Your will. I thank You for working in me as I decide to walk in health, and take action every day.*

*In Jesus' name I pray. Amen!*

# PUT OUT THE FIRE

*The tongue is a fire, a world of iniquity... and setteth on fire the course of nature; and it is set on fire of hell.*

—JAMES 3:6

SATAN HAS BEEN using our tongues to set on fire the course of nature against you and me. From the moment we were born into the world, we were trained to speak negatively about our life and circumstances around our life. The true source of the unruly evil produced by the tongue is hell. At one end the tongue spits deadly poison; at the other end it is manipulated by wicked spirits—therefore *no one* can tame it. You must use God the Father's Spirit to tame it. Train yourself to hear you own words. Do you speak casually, never thinking of how so-called casual remarks affect your life? Proverbs 6:2–3 says you are snared with the words of your mouth. You are taken by the words of your mouth.

**Read: James 3:2–12**

What is a little member and boasts great things? We bless our God and with it we curse men.

_____

_____

_____

Have you allowed the Holy Spirit to tame your little member?

_____

_____

_____

If so, how?

_____

_____

_____

What are some words you regularly speak that you should not?

_____

_____

_____

## *Let Us Pray!*

*Heavenly Father, thank You for helping me to walk by faith and not by sight. I have confidence in Your Word. Thank You for completing good work in me. Thank You. In Jesus' name I pray. Amen!*

# GREAT FAITH

J ESUS CALLED THE centurion's faith "great faith"! The centurion said to Jesus, "Speak the word only, and my servant shall be healed" (Matt. 8:8). Great faith is simply having faith in God's Word. God wants us to have the same faith as the centurion had. God wants us to have confidence in the authority of His Word. God is telling us to "Go thy way; and as thou hast believed, so be it done unto thee" (Matt. 8:13).

**Read: Matthew 8:5–13**

Are you speaking the Word only?

_____

_____

_____

What are you saying?

_____

_____

_____

Where is your faith?

_____

_____

_____

## *Let Us Pray!*

*Heavenly Father, I recognize by faith that God is worthy of all honor, praise, and worship as the Creator and Sustainer and End of all things. I recognize by faith that God loved me and chose me in Christ before time began, according to Ephesians 1:1–7. I recognize by faith that God has proven His love to me in sending His Son to die in my place, whereby every provision has already been made for my past, present, and future needs through His representative work whereby I have been quickened, raised, and seated with Christ the Anointed One (Rom. 5:6–11; 8:28–39). I recognize by faith that since I have received Christ as my Lord and Savior, I believe God's words when He says I am healed, delivered, and sanctified by the blood of Jesus Christ.*

*In Jesus' name I pray. Amen!*

# TAKE HEED IN WHAT YOU *HEAR* AND HOW YOU *SPEAK*

To have good health we must make a decision to take heed of what we hear and how we are hearing it. "If anyone has ears to hear, let him hear" (Matt. 11:15; 13:9, 43; Mark 4:9, 23; 7:16; Luke 8:8; 14:35).

> Take heed what you hear. With the same measure you use, it will be measured to you; and to you who hear, more will be given.
> —Mark 4:24, nkjv

The attention you give to God's Word produces power; power brings life, health, and healing to your body (Matt. 13:13–17; Luke 10:23–24).

How you hear the Word of God when you are facing a situation or trial (sickness) may become a Rhema word to you. (*Rhema*—a word spoken or given to you to stand on it, or walk in it—Eph. 6:13–20.)

*God always gives us a word before a situation comes. We must take heed when or how we hear it* (John 16:13).

God's words are anointed. The more we hear the Word the more it becomes faith. Faith comes to deliver us from the power of Satan and sickness. Your faith has made you well (Luke 8:48).

What are you saying about your healing? "I have read the scriptures on healing"; "I know God promised to heal me, but He hasn't done it yet"; "He was a minister and he stayed in the Word all the time, and he died last week with cancer"? (See Matthew 4:4; John 3:16.)

Remember, death and life are in the power of the tongue, and they that indulge it will eat the fruit of it (Prov. 18:21).

# WHAT ARE YOU SAYING?

*But I say to you that for every idle word men may speak,*
*they will give account of it in the Day of Judgment.*
—MATTHEW 12:36

MATTHEW 15:11 SAYS, "Not what goes into the mouth defiles a man; but what comes out of the mouth, this defiles a man" (NKJV).

> Pleasant words are like a honeycomb, sweetness to the soul and health to the bones. There is a way that seems right to a man, but its end is the way of death.
> —PROVERBS 16:24–25, NKJV

Wise words bring health.

> Let the words of my mouth and the meditation of my heart be acceptable in Your sight, O LORD, my strength and my Redeemer.
> —PSALM 19:14, NKJV

> The preparations of the heart belong to man, but the answer of the tongue is from the LORD.
> —PROVERBS 16:1, NKJV

**Read: James 3:1–6**

What is James saying?

_____

_____

_____

**Read: James 3:10**

What is James saying?

_____

_____

_____

## *Let Us Pray!*

*Heavenly Father, through Your Word You have imparted Your life to me. That life restores my body with every breath I breathe and every word I speak. First Peter 2:24 is engrafted into every fiber of my being and I am alive with the life of God. Every organ and every tissue of my body functions in the perfection in which God created it to function. I forbid any malfunction in my body.*

*In Jesus' name I pray. Amen!*

## DAY 11

# GUARD YOUR HEART

*Keep and guard your heart with all vigilance and above all that you guard, for out of it flow the springs of life.*
—Proverbs 4:23, amp

We guard our heart by keeping it full of the Word of God. That's the most important thing you have to do in life. We cannot live in divine health unless we keep a steady diet of the Word of God. The wisdom of God is written down for us in His Word. Revelation of the Word of God is precious because it takes care of everything in our life. It brings happiness, joy, and peace—nothing missing, nothing broken—*shalom*. *Shalom* means completeness, wholeness, well-being, and harmony.

**Read: Proverbs 3:1–18; Proverbs 4:20–27**

What are we to bind around our neck?

_____

_____

_____

We are to _____ the Lord with all our _____.

What will bring _____ to our flesh, and _____ to our bones?

_____

_____

_____

"My son, give _____ to my _____."

What should you keep in the midst of your heart?

_____

_____

_____

## *Let Us Pray!*

*Heavenly Father, thank You for helping me to walk by faith and not by sight. I have confidence in Your Word. Thank You for completing a good work in me.*

*In Jesus' name I pray. Amen!*

# YOUR DAYS OF SICKNESS AND DISEASE ARE OVER!

GOD WROTE IT in the blood covenant of His Son, Jesus Christ. God has shouted it down through the ages through prophets and apostles and preachers. "Surely [Jesus] hath borne our griefs [diseases] and carried our sorrows [pains]" (Isa. 53:4). The problem is most Christians have not let it reach down into their hearts and become truth to them. God has made His words plain to us. He said, "With His stripes we are healed" (Isa. 53:5). God always keeps His Word. Healing always comes! The problem has been in our receiving, not God's giving. It comes to those who will believe in their heart that Jesus was crucified and raised from the dead to purchase our healing. It comes to those who will open their mouths in faith and say that "By the stripes on Jesus Christ's back I am healed."

**Read: Matthew 15:21–31; Mark 6:53–56; Mark 7:31–37**

How did Jesus heal the deaf man's ears?

_____

_____

_____

How did Jesus heal the man's impediment of speech?

_____

_____

_____


Do you believe your days of sickness and disease are over?

_____

_____

_____


## *Let Us Pray!*

*Heavenly Father, thank You that I am born again by the incorruptible seed of the Word of God and I am free from the law of sin and death! I choose to live by Your Word, the Word that says I am free from sickness and disease. Thank You, Father God.*

*In Jesus' name I pray. Amen!*

# MAKE A DECLARATION OF FAITH

WHEN IT COMES to receiving from God, we must make a declaration of faith. Confess that Jesus is Lord over your life (Rom. 10:8–9). Humble yourself before the Lord (James 4:10). Lay the promises before God (1 John 5:15). Hear the wisdom and the instruction of the Holy Spirit (John 16:13).

**Read: Hebrews 10:35–36; Romans 4:16–21**

How does a declaration of faith set your faith in motion to receive?

_____

_____

_____

What promises from the Word minister to your situation?

_____

_____

_____

## Let Us Pray!

*Heavenly Father, it is written in Your Word in John 15:7–8 that if we abide in You and Your Word abides in us, we shall ask what we will and it shall be done for us. I thank You that we have received from Jesus Christ the victory over all diseases, affliction, infirmities, hindrances, persecution, torment, and lies that the enemy is trying to send our way now or in the future.*

*In Jesus' name I pray. Amen!*

# JESUS IS THE NAME THAT BRINGS HEALING

*O LORD, our Lord, How excellent is Your name in all the earth.*
**—PSALM 8:1, NKJV**

- Our names are precious to us...they reveal who we are.

- They are a personal connection, a unique part of us.

- Names in biblical times were very important, as they revealed a person's character.

- Some men are born to a great name, like kings; others make their name great by achievements.

JESUS' NAME IS great because He inherited and because of His great achievements. "And she shall bring forth a Son, and thou shalt call His name JESUS: for he shall save his people from their sins" (Matt. 1:21). The name *Jesus* is inseparably connected with salvation.

Jesus Christ—His glory—the Lord is Salvation—Son of Abraham (taking His royal lineage back to Abraham and Abrahamic Covenant.)

*Jesus* means Jehovah is Salvation, "is the Savior." God is salvation (Acts 8:16; 19:5).

- In the name of Jesus we can cast out demons (Luke 9:1).

- In the name of Jesus we are healed (Isa. 53:4–5).

- In the name of Jesus we can perform mighty miracles (Acts 3:6–9).

- In the name of Jesus we have power over sin, Satan, disease, death, and hell (Matt. 9:6; Heb. 2:14–15).

- We have the right to use the name of Jesus in our petitions in prayer (John 14:14).

# THERE'S HEALING IN THE NAME OF JESUS

WHEN YOU GET the revelation of the power and authority you have in the name of Jesus, no one can steal that revelation from you. You must use the name of Jesus in faith; otherwise, you will be ineffective and you will not get results.

Unbelievers cry and beg and plead, but believers speak with authority the name of Jesus and get results.

Through faith in the name of Jesus, you can exercise authority over the power of the enemy in your life and experience deliverance in healing.

**Read: Matthew 6:9–13; Philippians 2:9–11**

What must you have before the name of Jesus will produce results for you?

_____

_____

_____

Wherefore God also hath highly exalted _____ and given him a _____ which is above every name.

### Let Us Pray!

*Heavenly Father, the seed of Your Word is in my heart and being spoken out of my mouth. I see that Your will has always been for me to prosper and be in health, as my soul prospers. Thank You for what You have done for me.*

*In Jesus' name I pray. Amen!*

# PRAY TO THE FATHER IN
# THE NAME OF JESUS

YOU HAVE A right to ask for healing in the name of Jesus. God does hear and answer prayer. Every believer has a right to ask God the Father for healing, or for any other blessing in God's Word. When a believer asks in the name of Jesus, he has an absolute guarantee that God will grant him the answer to his petition. Under the new covenant between God and the church, we are to come to God by Jesus Christ.

> And in that day ye shall ask me nothing. Verily, verily, I say unto you, whatsoever ye shall ask the Father in My Name, He will give it to you. Until now you have asked nothing in My Name. Ask and you will receive, that your joy may be full.
>
> —JOHN 16:23–24

**Read: Psalm 50:15; Jeremiah 33:2–3; Matthew 7:7–11; John 5:7–9; John 9:7; 1 John 5:14–15**

According to John 16:23, what and why should you pray in Jesus' name?

_____

_____

_____

Under the new covenant between God and the church, how are we to come to God?

_____

_____

_____

### *Let Us Pray!*

*Heavenly Father, in the name of Jesus, I come before You asking You to heal me. It is written that the prayer of faith will save the sick, and the Lord will raise him up. Father God, my body is the temple of the Holy Spirit, and I desire to be healed. I seek wisdom that will make me free. Thank You, Father, for sending Your Word to heal me from all my destruction.*

*In Jesus' name I pray. Amen!*

# THERE'S HEALING POWER
# IN THE NAME OF JESUS

THE NAME OF Jesus belongs to you as a Christian, and you have the right to use it; but you need to know the power and authority of that name.

Jesus said, "And whatsoever ye shall ask in my name, that will I do, that the Father may be glorified in the Son. If ye shall ask any thing in my name, I will do it" (John 14:13–14).

In the early church, healing was used as a means to advertise the gospel as well as a means to bless and help people. Peter knew that there is power in the name of Jesus. Peter used the authority in that name to command sickness and disease to go.

**Read: Acts 3:1–16**

To whom does the name of Jesus belong?

_____

_____

_____

In Acts 3:2–8, when Peter demanded healing for the lame man in the name of Jesus, he didn't demand anything of God. To whom was he making the demand?

_____

_____

_____

### *Let Us Pray!*

*Heavenly Father, it is Your will for us to walk in health. Thank You for providing health and healing for us through the shed blood of Jesus on the cross. In the name of Jesus I speak total restoration to my body.*

*In Jesus' name I pray. Amen!*

# IT TAKES AN ACT OF OBEDIENCE
# TO RELEASE YOUR FAITH

WE MUST BELIEVE what the Scriptures are telling us. When the Scriptures told us that by the stripes of Jesus Christ we are healed, we must believe. The Bible tells us that we are a new creature, old things have passed away, we have become new inside and out. The Scriptures tell us to put away all filthiness and rampant outgrowth of naughtiness and receive the engrafted Word which is able to save us and bring healing to us (James 1:21–22, AMP).

Many times the Lord will tell you to do something, whisper a word into your ears—"Drink some water," "Don't eat that last piece of pie." Do we obey and stop eating or pick up a glass of water? Sometimes our body is telling us it needs something; do we stop to see what our body is telling us? When we are having a headache most of the time *our body is telling us to drink water.*

God told Naaman to go dip in the muddy Jordan (2 Kings 5:1–19). If Naaman had not obeyed, he would not have been healed.

When the Spirit of God tells someone to do a certain thing, it usually involves an act of obedience to release that person's faith. When God tells you to do something and you act upon it, you will be healed.

Be obedient to the Word (Deut. 30:19–20; Heb. 10:35–39; Ezek. 36:26–28; Ps. 34:1–22).

# YOU HAVE A PART TO PLAY

IN CHAPTER 9 of Mark's Gospel, a man came running up to Jesus telling Him about his son, who was possessed by a demon that tried to convince the boy to throw himself into fire and water. The disciples had been unable to deliver the boy, so the father begged Jesus, saying, "If thou canst do anything, have compassion on us, and help us" (Mark 9:22). Jesus replied, "If thou canst *believe*, all things are possible to him that *believeth*" (Mark 9:23, emphasis added). In James 2:14, Jesus brought to the man's attention that faith *without works* is dead. Jesus immediately started working on the man's ability to believe, which had to do with his spirit. Jesus turned the father's plea for help around and said, "It's not a matter of what I can do. It's matter of what you believe."

**Read: Matthew 8:5–10; Matthew 9:27–30**

What did all these people have in common?

_____

_____

_____

How does God heal?

_____

_____

_____

### *Let Us Pray!*

*Heavenly Father, I ask You to heal me of _____, _____, and _____ in Jesus' name according to Your Word. Sickness and disease have no power over me. You have given me abundant life and I receive it through Your Word. Your Word flows to every organ of my body, bringing life. I speak healing over my body, according to John 10:10 and John 6:63.*

*In Jesus' name I pray. Amen!*

# WHO'S CALLING THE SHOTS?

THIS DESTITUTE WOMAN reached out in faith to touch the hem of Jesus' garment—the woman with the issue of blood. Her faith brought the power of God into her body. Notice how she said what she believed. For she said, "If I may touch but His clothes, I shall be whole" (Mark 5:28). When she touched Him, she released her faith and received her healing, just like she said (Mark 5:25–34). The lady with the issue of blood declared her faith and how she would receive her healing. Who was calling the shots? Jesus did not call the shots, the woman did. Her faith did. It's still the same today. Through the Word of God, and by faith, decree healing into your life and your children's lives. The scripture tells us if we believe, we receive when we pray, and we will have whatsoever we say (Mark 11:24).

**Read: Mark 11:20–26; Matthew 7:7–8; John 14:1, 12–14**

Who's calling your shots?

_____

_____

_____

For everyone who asks _____, and he who _____ _____, and to him who _____ it will be opened.

What is Mark 11:20–24 telling us to do?

_____

_____

_____

### *Let Us Pray!*

*Heavenly Father, I have confidence in Your Word, and I take hold of Your promises to heal me. According to Isaiah 53:5 and 1 Peter 2:24, I resist sickness and disease. I speak with my mouth and believe in my heart that I am healed of all sickness and disease.*

*In Jesus' name I pray. Amen!*

# KNOW WITHIN YOURSELF

*We must know within ourselves what we have been given in Jesus. That means we must know it not just with our head but with our heart. We must have His Word rooted so deeply and firmly within us that when we hear lies to the contrary, we don't buy them.... [Satan] can really paint a bleak picture. He can whisper negative thoughts in your ear and make your situation look so bad that you may find yourself wanting to quit....We must be so fully persuaded of what God says that we act as if it's true even when natural circumstances look like it's not. We cannot quit when the going gets tough. If we quit, it's over. If we lay down our faith and give up, the devil can keep us in permanent defeat. On the other hand, we will win if we don't quit [Heb. 10:35–38].*

—GLORIA COPELAND[1]

[Not in your own strength] for it is God Who is all the while effectually at work in you [energizing and creating in you the power and desire], both to will and to work for His good pleasure and satisfaction and delight.

—PHILIPPIANS 2:13, AMP

**Read: Philippians 4:6–9; Ephesians 6:10–17; Hebrews 10:23**

In order to keep the devil away from you, what does Ephesians 6:11 tell you to do?

_____

_____

_____

Ephesians 6:14 tells you to have _____ your _____

with _____.

What things does Philippians 4:8 tell you to meditate on?

_____

_____

_____

_____

_____

## *Let Us Pray!*

*Father, I know You have already made salvation and healing available to me by Your Word. I choose now to receive from You all that You have for me. I choose to believe You rather than my circumstances. Thank You for helping me to stand strong.*

*In Jesus' name I pray. Amen!*

# TAKE A STAND FOR YOUR HEALING

T HE THIEF, SATAN, comes only to steal, kill, and destroy. Jesus came that we might have life and have it more abundantly (John 10:10). We the believers must decide not to back up any longer. Here Jesus is giving us the real possibility of health for our total body, mind, emotions, and relationship. Jesus said that He came to give life—not just ordinary existence, but a life of fullness, abundance, and prosperity. On the other hand, the enemy (Satan) came only to steal (your good health), kill (your joy), and to destroy (your body). The line is clearly drawn. One side is God with goodness, life, and plenty; and on the other side is Satan, who comes to rob us of God's blessings, to oppress our bodies with sickness and disease. We take a stand (John 10:10).

**Read: Ephesians 6:13–14; 1 Thessalonians 3:8; 1 Peter 5:12**

Make a list of the things you need to stand for and a list you need to stand against.

_____        _____

_____        _____

_____        _____

_____        _____

_____        _____

What is Satan trying to get you to back up from?

_____

_____

_____

_____

_____

### *Let Us Pray!*

*Heavenly Father, it is written in Your Word in John 15:7–8 that if I abide in You and Your Word abides in me, I shall ask what I will and it shall be done for me. So that You, my Heavenly Father, will be glorified and I will bear much fruit. I pray, Father God, that You will give me total healing, total deliverance from all sickness, diseases of any kind, and that all the organs in my body, every tissue, every cell, every gland, muscle, and every bone in my body will function according to the way You designed them to work.*

*In Jesus' name I pray. Amen!*

# REBUKE THE STORM

*Now it happened, on a certain day that Jesus got into a boat
with His disciples. And Jesus said to them: "Let us cross
over to the other side of the lake." But as they sailed, Jesus
fell asleep. A windstorm came down on the lake the boat
was filling with water, they were in jeopardy. They came
to Jesus and woke Him, saying "Master, we are perishing!"
Then Jesus arose and rebuked the wind and the raging of
the water. The storm ceased, and there was a calm.*

—LUKE 8:22–25

PEOPLE ALWAYS BLAME God for the storms, catastrophes, earth-
quakes, and floods that occur in their lives, but Satan is the
cause.

> How God anointed Jesus of Nazareth with the Holy
> Ghost and with power: who went about doing good deeds
> and healing all that were oppressed of the devil.
>
> —ACTS 10:38

**Read: Matthew 8:23–27; Psalm 107:27–32**

Do you believe that God can rebuke the storms in your life?

What will it take to believe God in your storms?

_____

_____

_____

Who causes the storms in your life?

_____

## *Let Us Pray!*

*Heavenly Father, it is written in John 15:7–8 that if Your Word abides in me, Lord Jesus, and I abide in You, I shall ask what I will and it shall be done for me, so that Your Father in heaven will be glorified. So I ask You, Lord Jesus, to heal me of every disease, every infirmity, every inflammation, and of every affliction.*

*In Jesus' name I pray. Amen!*

# WE'VE ALREADY BEEN
# REDEEMED FROM SICKNESS

- Jesus has already suffered for you, and bore your grief (*to make sick*)

- Satan is trying every day to make us sick

- Jesus carried our sorrows (*our burdens*)

- Jesus has already redeemed us (*paid the price*), just like someone paying for your meal. Do you stand around eating off another person's plate, or do you get your own plate and eat?

- Isaiah 53:4–5; Matthew 8:17; 1 Peter 2:24

- Jesus has *destroyed* the works of the devil—all of his works. According to 1 John 3:8, *Jesus redeemed the whole man.*

- Understanding the truth of God's Word concerning healing will destroy Satan's grip on your life.

- Remember there is no disease so devastating to the human body that the sacrifice at Calvary will not cancel it and wipe it out.

- As the body of Christ, we do not have to tolerate sickness or disease any longer.

# GOD'S REDEMPTIVE PLAN

JESUS NOT ONLY redeemed us from sin, He also redeemed us from sickness. So it is God's will to heal you. Never doubt it, because healing is in His redemptive plan. Jesus sealed the new covenant with His blood, so we have a legal right to His divine healing (Heb. 8:6; 12:24; 13:20). The new covenant guarantees us the rights and privileges that Jesus secured for us. In Mark 11:24 He said, "What things soever ye desire, when ye pray, believe that ye receive them, and ye shall have them."

**Read: Romans 8:1–28**

Who has the right to be healed?

_____

_____

_____

Proverbs 4:20 says, "Incline thine ear unto my saying." Why?

_____

_____

_____

## Let Us Pray!

*Heavenly Father, I worship You, I give You reverence. I confess with my mouth that Your Word will not return to You void. I praise You for Your protection and for Your goodness upon my life. Your Word says whatever I ask in Your name, it will be done for me. I declare that sickness, disease, and pain will not be lord over me anymore. I resist you in the name of Jesus. You are not the will of God for my life. I enforce the Word of God on you. I will not tolerate you in my life. Leave my presence now.*

*In Jesus' name I pray. Amen!*

# THE ONLY WAY TO LIVE

SOME PEOPLE ARE reluctant to receive their healing by faith. They think it's too hard to do. So they just go to the doctor or wait around hoping someone will lay hands on them and zap them with the power of God, in spite of their unbelief. Jesus paid the price for our healing with His blood. He paid the debt we owed to God for every sinful thing we have done or will ever do. Jesus set us free from sin, sickness, and pain. He paid the bill so we can be whole—in spirit, soul, and body (Isa. 53:4–5). We must have faith to receive. Faith simply believes what God says in His Word and trusts what God says more than our natural senses or the doctor's report. We increase our faith by hearing the Word of God. Spend more time in the Word of God (Rom. 10:17).

**Read: Hebrews 11:1–21**

What is faith?

_____

_____

_____

Without _____ it is _____ to please Him.

"By faith Sarah herself also _____ _____ to conceive."

If you were arrested for having faith, what would be the evidence against you?

_____

_____

_____

### *Let Us Pray!*

*Heavenly Father, I release my faith now, as I speak that by Jesus' stripes I am healed, and confess my total healing from the top of my head to the soles of my feet. My words will come to pass, and I believe that I have my healing now.*

*In Jesus' name I pray. Amen!*

# HEALING IS HIS CHILDREN'S BREAD

THESE ARE JESUS' own words; you can incline your ear to the fact that healing is your bread. That means if you are born again, then you're God's child, and healing belongs to you. The Word has a lot to say about divine healing. Read God's Word and you will find life and health (John 6:63).

> I am the bread of life. Your fathers ate the manna in the wilderness, and are dead. This is the bread which comes down from heaven, that one may eat of it and not die. I am the living bread which came down from heaven. If anyone eats of this bread, he will live forever; and the bread that I shall give is My flesh, which I shall give for the life of the world.
>
> —JOHN 6:48–51, NKJV

**Read: John 1:14–16; John 6:35, 41, 58; 1 Corinthians 10:1–3; Exodus 15:26; Exodus 16:4**

What is the bread of life?

_____

_____

_____

How can we live forever?

_____

_____

_____

## *Let Us Pray!*

*Father, I see how religious tradition, double-minded-ness, and discouragement can keep me from walking in Your life and health. But I choose life, and I know Your grace is sufficient for me. Your truth has made me free. Thank You, Lord.*

*In Jesus' name I pray. Amen!*

# SO GREAT OF A PRICE!

THE ENGLISH LANGUAGE does not clearly communicate to us what the word *salvation* (or the Greek word *sozo*) really means. It's not just the new birth of your spirit. It's also peace for your mind and healing for your body. There is no price greater than Jesus' sacrifice at Calvary. What a price! Jesus came to destroy the works of the devil—*all* of his works (1 John 3:8). He did not destroy sin only to leave sickness in dominion. Partial redemption from Satan's power would not have pleased God, nor would it have fulfilled His plan for His family. He redeemed the whole man—righteousness for his nature, peace for his mind, and healing for his body. Redemption left nothing in play that came on man as a result of sin. Jesus completely destroyed the works of the devil in our lives. What a great price He paid (1 Cor. 6:20; Matt. 16:18–21).

**Read: Matthew 14:13–16; John 3:16–17**

What is the new birth?

_____

_____

_____

The power of God cleanses and changes anyone who receives salvation until there is no trace of the old man or his sin. Have you allowed the new man to come into your life?

_____

What do the words "old man" mean?

_____

_____

_____

What was the price you were bought with?

_____

_____

_____

## Let Us Pray!

_Heavenly Father, I thank You that I am born again by the incorruptible seed of the Word of God and free from the law of sin and death. I choose to live by Your Word, and I trust You to help me grow and mature._

_In Jesus' name I pray. Amen!_

# THE GIFT OF HEALING

THE FAITH BY which you are saved is a gift of God. It is given to you through hearing the Word. "Faith cometh by hearing, and hearing by the Word of God" (Rom. 10:17). The gift of faith is a gift of the Spirit to the believer, that he might receive a miracle, whereas the working of miracles is a gift of the Spirit to the believer that he might work a miracle. The gifts of healing and faith go hand in hand. The gift of faith and healing is a unique form of faith that goes beyond natural faith and healing. If we supernaturally trust and do not doubt, God will supernaturally heal us by the Spirit, totally removing all sickness, diseases, and any disorders from us. For the gifts and the calling of God are irrevocable (Rom. 11:29; Mark 6:13; 16:18).

**Read: Hebrews 11:1–11; Hebrews 12:12–13**

Some have mistakenly thought that the gifts of healing refer to the fact that God has given us doctors and medical science. What do you think?

_____

_____

_____

## Let Us Pray!

*Heavenly Father, in the name of Jesus, I pray that the will of God be done in my life as it is in heaven. Father God, I am Your own handiwork, recreated in Christ Jesus, born anew in your Spirit that I should walk in the good life You have prearranged and made ready for me. Teach me Your will; lead me into a plain country and into a land of health and healing.*

*In Jesus' name I pray. Amen!*

# SICKNESS IS OF THE DEVIL

*And the LORD said to Satan, "From where do you come?"*
*Satan answered the Lord and said, "From going to and fro*
*on the earth, and from walking back and forth on it."*

—JOB 2:2, NKJV

SATAN IS ALWAYS trying to prove that we serve God for what
we can get. Satan indicates God's claims of Job's righteousness
were untested, so Job's relationship with God was a sham. Satan
was confident that he could turn Job against God. Satan thought
he could destroy Job's faith in God by inflicting suffering and sickness on him; but God's saving faith cannot be shattered or broken.
Job's faith in God never failed.

Satan tried to do the same to Peter (Luke 22:31–34), but was
unsuccessful in destroying Peter's faith (John 21:15–19). When
Satan unleashed all that he had, he still could not destroy Job's nor
Peter's faith; it always stood firm (Rom. 8:31–39).

**Read: Job 2:1–10**

What would you do in Job's situation?

_____

_____

_____

_____

_____

### *Let Us Pray!*

*Heavenly Father, thank You for sending Your Word to heal me and deliver me from all destructions. Jesus, You bore my griefs (pains) and carried my sorrows (sickness). My body is the temple of the Holy Spirit, and I desire to be in good health.*

*In Jesus Christ's name I pray. Amen!*

# BREAKING GENERATIONAL CURSES

BY DEFINITION, A generational curse is "an uncleansed iniquity that increases in strength from one generation to the next, affecting the members of that family and all who come into relationship with that family."[1]

> I the LORD thy God am a jealous God, visiting the iniquity
> of the fathers upon the children unto the third and fourth
> generation of them that hate me.
>
> —EXODUS 20:5

The origin of generational curses started with Adam, when he disobeyed God's command to not eat of the tree of good and evil. Not only did it affect his family, but every family that came after him (Gen. 3:16–18).

The Bible makes a distinction between the terms *sin, iniquity, and transgression:*

- *Sin* means (Greek and Hebrew) to miss the mark from what God called you to do (Rom. 3:23).

- *Transgression* means to trespass against man and God. To overstep pre-established boundaries. Example: violate a NO TRESPASSING sign, entering onto someone's property without permission.

- *Iniquity* means to bend or to distort (the heart); to commit a certain sin over and over again. That sin becomes an iniquity and that sin can be passed down through the bloodline. Your children become weak to the same sin. An iniquity can compared to a bruise, because it stays around and goes to the bone from generation to generation, like hurts (family, friends and love ones), we must beware the bruises (Matt. 7:15–17).

Every seed reproduces after its own kind. Within every seed there is inherent ability inseparable element to reproduce itself. In other words, sins are passed down through your bloodline. A generation of alcohol or a generation of stealing will be passed down unless a member of the family stops drinking or stealing, and changes the way he or she lives (Gen. 1:11–12).

# RENEWING OF YOUR MIND

M AKE A DECISION to *dedicate* your bodies, presenting all your members and faculties to God.

> I beseech you therefore, brethren, by the mercies of God, that ye present your *bodies* a living sacrifice, holy, acceptable unto God, which is your *reasonable service.* And be not conformed to this world: but be ye transformed by the renewing of your mind, that ye may prove what is that good, and acceptable, and perfect, will of God.
>                           —ROMANS 12:1–2, EMPHASIS ADDED

For us to be healed, we need to reach out for a new level of understanding and comprehension concerning the power of God to heal our bodies.

**Read: 1 Corinthians 2:1–9**

List some of the things God has prepared for us.

_____

_____

_____

What does the word *convert* mean?

_____

_____

_____

## *Let Us Pray!*

*Heavenly Father, I attend to Your Word, I incline my ears to Your sayings. I will not let them depart from my eyes. I will keep them in the midst of my heart, for they are life and healing to all my flesh. Therefore, I will not allow any sickness to dominate my body. The life of God flows within me, bringing healing and restoring life to me.*

*In Jesus Christ's name I pray. Amen!*

# LIFE UNDER THE SUN OR
# LIFE UNDER THE S-O-N

EVERYONE UNDER THE sun is subject to all kinds of affliction and ailments, but all these things have to melt away when we live in the light of the S-O-N. That is God's Son, the Lord Jesus Christ! In the Book of Ecclesiastes, Solomon kept using the phrase, "Life under the sun is vanity." King Solomon tried to prove to himself that the world was better, this "wisest" of all men, but he only found vanity; his search was all in vain (Eccles. 1:12–14). We don't have to live and die under the sun; we can live under the S-O-N (Deut. 30:19–20). You will not always be happy, you will encounter grief and pain, but you can always have the joy of the Lord, which is your strength. You should be expecting divine health from living under the S-O-N (James 3:13–17).

**Read: Deuteronomy 28:1–19**

Under the sun or under the S-O-N—where do you want to be?

What do you need to do to be where you want to be?

---

_____

_____

_____

### *Let Us Pray!*

*Heavenly Father, I ask You to put a hedge of protection around me in the name of Jesus. I apply the blood of Jesus over every organ, every cell, every gland, muscle, ligament, and bone in my body. I ask You to restore health and healing to my body.*

*In Jesus' name I pray. Amen!*

# THE NEW BREED

J ESUS IS NOT coming back for a weak, sickly church that has been defeated and beaten down by Satan. "Let us walk properly, as in the day, not in revelry and drunkenness, not in lewdness and lust, not in strife and envy. But put on the Lord Jesus Christ, and make no provision for the flesh, to fulfill its lusts" (Rom. 13:13–14, NKJV). Then, you will be walking in the fullness of God, miraculous power will take place, and you will be counted as a "new breed."

**Read: Galatians 5:1–26**

How shall we walk?

_____

_____

_____

What is it you should not do?

_____

_____

_____

## Let Us Pray!

*Father, I choose to stand firm in Your peace. I thank You for helping me to walk by faith and not by sight. I have all confidence in You and Your Word that the work You have started in me, You are able to finish.*

*In Christ Jesus' name I pray. Amen!*

# TAKE DOMINION OVER YOUR BODY

*If any man offend not in word, the same is a perfect man, and able also to bridle the whole body.*

—JAMES 3:2

TO TAKE DOMINION means to curb, control, and restrain. I discipline my body like an athlete, training it to do what it should. Keep it under control. The body will respond to the commands of the human spirit. Speak to your body and tell it to obey God's Word; do not let your body tell you what to do. Take dominion over your body in the same way Adam was to take dominion over the earth (1 Cor. 9:27; Rom. 8:12–13).

**Read: Romans 6:1–23**

What do we need to take control of?

_____

_____

_____

How do we put to death the deeds of the body?

_____

_____

_____

### *Let Us Pray!*

*Heavenly Father, I ask You to give me divine health and healing in Jesus' name according to Your Word in John 16:23. I forbid the enemy from trying to steal my healing. I bind my mind with the mind of Jesus; I bring every thought captive to the obedience of Jesus Christ. Father God, overflow me with Your Holy Spirit.*

*In Jesus' name I pray, Amen!*

# FEEDING YOUR SPIRIT CONTINUALLY

*He sent His Words, and healed them and deliv-
ered them from their destructions.*
—PSALM 107:20

- Healing is God's nature.

- The Lord is full of compassion.

- The Lord will keep you free from every disease.

- The Lord will restore health unto you (Matt. 4:4; Mark 5:35–36; Isa. 55:3).

- God does not hold back. He's not misleading (Ps. 91:14–16).

- The power of God will be poured out on us as we continue to read His Word.

- The more we feed on His Word, the more we are like Him.

# LOOKING INTO THE HEART OF GOD

PERHAPS YOU HAVE been troubled and sought help or counsel from a spiritual friend. Maybe you have heard the advice, "Seek the face of God." Many people throughout history have wanted to see God's face. In the Bible we read about people who "sought the face of God." Why? Because when you can look at someone's face, you can also see what's in their heart. And the same is true with God; if you see His face, you see His heart. When you are seeking, it helps greatly if you know what your goal is and what you'll find once you are there. You see, our true seeking always begins with worshipping God. That is how we acknowledge Him as the source of all we need (healing). No matter where we are in our seeking, God wants us to come nearer to Him. Then, even if we still feel we are at a distance from God, He reveals His love to us (Deut. 4:29–31; 2 Chron. 19:3; Ps. 9:1–2).

**Read: 2 Chronicles 7:14–15; Matthew 6:27–34; Matthew 7:7–11**

What do these scriptures tell you?

_____

_____

_____

When you look into the heart of God, what do you see?

_____

_____

_____

## *Let Us Pray!*

*Heavenly Father, I ask You to give me divine healing now in every area of my life, spirit, mind, will, and emotions, and keep me in accordance with Your divine plan for my life.*

*In Jesus' name I pray. Amen!*

# POSSESS THE LAND

AFTER YOU HAVE received God's Word for healing by faith, begin to do what you couldn't do before. James 1:22 says we must be doers of the Word, not hearers only. The children of Israel in the wilderness are good examples of what happens to *hearers* who are not *doers*. Through Moses, God told this nation of people He had given them the land. At one point, Moses basically told them the Lord said they had been going around the same mountain long enough (Deut. 1:6). Have you ever felt like that? Perhaps even now you are going around that mountain of unbelief and getting nowhere fast! If so, you can take drastic faith action! What God said to the children of Israel applies to you as well. He said: "Behold, I have set the land before you: *go in and possess the land* which the Lord sware unto your fathers... to give unto them and to their seed after them" (v. 8, emphasis added). God had promised them the land. But possessing it wasn't automatic. He was telling them to go armed and *take it*. That was the only way they were going to get it. *If you need healing*, that's how you must possess it too! You must take it! *Take it by force* (Matt. 11:12)!

**Read: James 1:22; Mark 11:23–24; 2 Corinthians 4:18; Deuteronomy 31:6–8**

Why is James telling us to be doers of the Word?

_____

_____

_____

What is Deuteronomy 31:6 telling you to do?

_____

_____

_____

Therefore I say to you, whatever things you _____ when you _____, _____ that you _____ them, and you _____ _____ them.

## *Let Us Pray!*

*Heavenly Father, I choose to operate in the life that You have given me and to let love rule my heart. Thanks for healing me.*

*In Jesus' name I pray. Amen!*

# LOOK WHAT THE LORD HAS DONE!

As you read through the Gospels, you'll find that Jesus took our sin, sickness, and disease, and on the third day He arose! He overcame hell and death, totally destroying Satan's power. Colossians 2:15 says: "Having spoiled principalities and power, He made a [show] of them openly, triumphing over them in it."

> For this purpose the Son of God was manifested, that he might destroy the works of the devil.
>
> —1 John 3:8

**Read: James 4:7; Matthew 28:18–19; John 10:10–11**

We must _____ to God, _____ the devil, and he will _____.

"All _____ has been given to me."

How can we apply Matthew 28:18–19 to us today?

_____

_____

_____

What have you allowed Satan to take from you?

_____

_____

_____

How can you get it back?

_____

_____

_____

## *Let Us Pray!*

*Christ has redeemed me from the curse of the law. I forbid any sickness or disease to come upon this body. Every disease, germ, and virus that touches my body dies instantly.*

*In Jesus' name I pray. Amen!*

# LET GO OF THE DOUBT

*God anointed Jesus of Nazareth with the Holy Ghost and with power: who went about doing good, and healing all that were oppressed of the devil; for God was with him.*
—ACTS 10:38

Did Jesus just heal some? No. Jesus healed all who were oppressed of the devil.

In Mark 6:5–6, the people in Nazareth did not believe Jesus because they knew Him and where He came from; they knew His parents. The Word said Jesus could not do any great works in Nazareth because of their unbelief. Doubt will rob you of God's blessings. Unbelief will rob you and leave you sick. There is only one thing that can stop doubt and unbelief in the heart of a man, and that is the Word of God. When a person receives the Word, doubt, defeat, and discouragement have to leave (Num. 23:19–20; Matt. 21:21).

**Read: Exodus 23:25–26; Psalm 103:1–5**

How can you combat doubt and unbelief?

_____

_____

_____

Jesus could not do great works and heal the people in what city?

_____

Why?

_____

_____

_____

## Let Us Pray!

*Heavenly Father, I thank You that I believe Your Word that You took all my sins and sickness on the cross. And thank You that I am already healed, because I believe, I receive it now. Your living Word, Jesus, is powerful and working in me right now.*

*In Jesus' name I pray. Amen!*

# THINGS THAT BLOCK HEALING

God never holds out on us. His will is that all men be healed—and that includes you! Jesus purchased your healing at the same time He purchased your redemption from sin (Isa. 53:4–5). Health is just as available to you as salvation. When we fail to receive something He's promised, we can always be assured that the problem lies with us and not with Jesus. There are several things that prevent us from receiving healing. Walk in the Spirit, and ye shall not fulfill the lust of the flesh.

> For the flesh lusteth against the Spirit, and the Spirit against the flesh: and these are contrary the one to the other: so that ye cannot do the things that ye would. But if ye be led of the Spirit, ye are not under the law. Now the works of the flesh are manifest, which are these; Adultery, fornication, uncleanness, lasciviousness, idolatry, witchcraft, hatred, variance, emulations, wrath, strife, seditions, heresies, envyings, murders, drunkenness, revellings, and such like: of the which I tell you before, as I have also told you in time past, that they which do such things shall not inherit the kingdom of God.
>
> —GALATIANS 5:17–21

**Read: Matthew 22:37–40; Mark 11:24–26; Galatians 5:1–26**

Please list what's blocking your healing.

_____

_____

_____

What will you do about the things that are blocking your healing?

_____

_____

_____

## Let Us Pray!

*Thank You, Father, for helping me to escape the cor-ruption in this present world by Your divine nature that is in me. I choose to operate in the life that You have given me, and to let love rule in my heart. Thank You that I am healed.*

*In Jesus' name I pray. Amen!*

# REFUSE TO OWN SICKNESS

MANY HAVE ACTUALLY allowed sickness to become their identity. John 5 tells the story of a man who owned his sickness for thirty-eight years. The Bible says that he lay at the pool in Bethesda among a great multitude of sick people, blind, lame, and paralyzed, waiting for an angel to stir up the water. The first person to step into the water after it was stirred was made well.

> When Jesus saw him lying there, and knew that he already had been in that condition a long time, He said to him, "Do you want to be made well?" The sick man answered Him, "Sir I have no man to put me into the pool when the water is stirred up; but while I am coming, another steps down before me." Jesus said to him, "Rise, take up your bed and walk." And immediately the man was made well, took up his bed, and walked.
>
> —JOHN 5:6–9, NKJV

**Read: John 5:2–9; Luke 13:10–13; Luke 8:43–48**

Do you own/accept your sickness?

What could the man at the pool have done?

_____

_____

_____

What would you have done if it was you who lay sick at the pool?

_____

_____

_____

## Let Us Pray!

_Heavenly Father, give me deliverance and freedom from all these bondages in the name of Christ Jesus according to John 16:33. Deliver me from a life of sickness, affliction, diseases, iniquities, trespasses, and transgressions._

_In Jesus' name I pray. Amen!_

# THE TREE OF LIFE

*And he shewed me a pure river of water of life, clear as crystal,
proceeding out of the throne of God and of the Lamb. In the
midst of the street of it, and on either side of the river, was
there the tree of life, which bare twelve manner of fruits, and
yielded her fruit every month: and the leaves of the tree
were for the healing of the nations....Blessed are they that
do his commandments, that they may have right to the tree
of life, and may enter in through the gates into the city.*
—REVELATION 22:1–2, 14

THE TREE OF life was used to sustain eternal life and healing for
God's people. God's plan was for man to live free from sickness and death. When He made the earth, God put everything
man would need to keep him alive and well. Think about it; the
leaves on the tree of life were for healing. But because of man's fall,
sickness came.

**Read: Genesis 2:9; Proverbs 11:30; Revelation 2:7**

If you eat the right foods and read the Word of God, you will have
good health and life. Eat the wrong foods, say the wrong things,
you will have sickness and death (Prov. 12:12–14).

What are you eating?

_____

_____

_____

What are you saying?

_____

_____

_____

## *Let Us Pray!*

*Father God, thank You for the tree of life that brings healing to my body. Thank You for Your Word that brings eternal life. Jesus took my infirmities and bore my sickness. Therefore I refuse to allow sickness to dominate my body, in Jesus' name. Amen.*

# A LIVING SACRIFICE

WHEN YOU LIVE to please God, you will not be squeezed into the world's mold. You'll be transformed into the image of Jesus. Today is the day to offer your body as a living sacrifice to God. You do not have to fight the war between your flesh and spirit. Instead, lay down your desires to fulfill your flesh, so you can fulfill God's desires (Rom. 12:1–2). God is calling us to give ourselves to Him (John 12:26). We cannot serve the flesh and serve Jesus at the same time. We must make a decision—are you going to please yourself or the Father? We are to crucify our flesh and bring it into obedience to God.

**Read: Romans 12:1–2; Ephesians 4:22–32; Ephesians 5:1–21**

What does Romans 12 mean when it defines "reasonable service" as offering our bodies as a living sacrifice?

_____

_____

_____

What are some of the things Ephesians 4 tells us to do or put away from us?

_____

_____

_____

How shall we be imitators of God?

_____

_____

_____

How shall we walk?

_____

_____

_____

## *Let Us Pray!*

*Father God, help me to escape the corruption in this present evil world by walking in the Spirit and not in the flesh, to choose life and not death and healing over sickness, and to believe in You.*

*In Jesus' name I pray. Amen!*

# GOD'S GREAT MERCY

*The LORD is gracious, and full of compassion; slow to anger, and of great mercy. The LORD is good to all: and his tender mercies are over all his works.*

—PSALM 145:8–9

NOTHING REVEALS THE character of God more than these two scriptures. If you look up the words *compassion* and *mercy*, you will find the Hebrew or Greek word translates *compassion* as "mercy" and *mercy* as "compassion." Therefore, to have mercy means to have compassion! God is full of compassion; He is of great mercy and His tender mercies are over all of His works.

**Read: Mark 1:40–45**

List other ways Jesus showed compassion.

_____

_____

_____

_____

_____

Is God still merciful?

---

### *Let Us Pray!*

*Dear Father God, I receive Your mercy and compassion to heal me. I am the saved, I am the healed. The power of sickness over my life has been forever broken. Jesus bore my sickness, my weakness, and pain. Therefore, I am free and I am redeemed from the curse. I receive Your blessing and I proclaim my freedom.*

*In Jesus' name I pray. Amen!*

# NOTES

## Day 19: Know Within Yourself

1. Gloria Copeland, "A Future Full of God's Promises," Kenneth Copeland Ministries, http://www.kcm.org/real-help/article/future-full-gods-promises (accessed April 24, 2013).

## Lesson Seven: Breaking Generational Curses

1. Marilyn Hickey, *Breaking Generational Curses* (Tulsa, OK: Harrison House, 2000), 13.

# ABOUT THE AUTHOR

ETHELENE PATTERSON STANLEY is married to Minister John D. Stanley, and has been blessed with three beautiful girls and four grandchildren. She loves to serve the body of Christ in any way she can, and her passion is teaching the Word of God. She taught for over eight years in the teen ministry and over six years in children's ministry. Ethelene has spoken at several women's ministries and conferences. She also owns and operates several businesses (EPS Tax Services, CJS Janitorial Service, and Keeping It On the Road driving school), where she uses the interaction with her clients as an opportunity to be a witness of God's love. She helps single moms re-enter the work force by training them in her tax services. Currently, Ethelene is conducting a series of classes on healing, using this book as a guidance tool for her lessons.

# CONTACT THE AUTHOR

*E-mail:*

ethelene53@gmail.com